# BACKYARD HABITATS

Introducing Habitats

## Kelley MacAulay and Bobbie Kalman

🍄 Crabtree Publishing Company

www.crabtreebooks.com

# Created by Bobbie Kalman

Dedicated by Kelley MacAulay
For Sue Philp, my friend on the Path and the trails!

**Editor-in-Chief**
Bobbie Kalman

**Writing team**
Kelley MacAulay
Bobbie Kalman

**Substantive editor**
Kathryn Smithyman

**Editors**
Molly Aloian
Michael Hodge
Rebecca Sjonger

**Design**
Margaret Amy Salter
Samantha Crabtree
(cover and series logo)

**Production coordinator**
Heather Fitzpatrick

**Photo research**
Crystal Foxton

**Special thanks to**
Jack Pickett and Karen Van Atte

**Illustrations**
Barbara Bedell: page 32 (top and bottom)
© Crabtree Publishing Company: pages 10, 11
Bonna Rouse: pages 8-9, 15, 32 (middle)

**Photographs**
© Can Stock Photo Inc.: page 24 (left)
Other images by Corel, Creatas, Digital Stock, Digital Vision,
Eyewire, and Photodisc

**Library and Archives Canada Cataloguing in Publication**

MacAulay, Kelley
    Backyard habitats / Kelley MacAulay & Bobbie Kalman.
(Introducing habitats)
Includes index.
ISBN-13: 978-0-7787-2957-0 (bound)
ISBN-10: 0-7787-2957-5 (bound)
ISBN-13: 978-0-7787-2985-3 (pbk.)
ISBN-10: 0-7787-2985-0 (pbk.)
    1. Urban ecology--Juvenile literature. I. Kalman, Bobbie, date.
II. Title. III. Series.

QH541.5.C6M32 2006    j577.5'6    C2006-904096-6

**Library of Congress Cataloging-in-Publication Data**

MacAulay, Kelley.
    Backyard habitats / Kelley MacAulay & Bobbie Kalman.
     p. cm. -- (Introducing habitats)
Includes index.
ISBN-13: 978-0-7787-2957-0 (rlb)
ISBN-10: 0-7787-2957-5 (rlb)
ISBN-13: 978-0-7787-2985-3 (pb)
ISBN-10: 0-7787-2985-0 (pb)
    1. Urban ecology--Juvenile literature. I. Kalman, Bobbie. II. Title.
QH541.5.C6M27 2007
577.5'6--dc22
                                2006018059

## Crabtree Publishing Company

www.crabtreebooks.com    1-800-387-7650

**Published in Canada**
**Crabtree Publishing**
616 Welland Ave.
St. Catharines, ON
L2M 5V6

**Published in the United States**
**Crabtree Publishing**
PMB16A
350 Fifth Ave., Suite 3308
New York, NY 10118

**Published in the United Kingdom**
**Crabtree Publishing**
White Cross Mills
High Town, Lancaster
LA1 4XS

**Published in Australia**
**Crabtree Publishing**
386 Mt. Alexander Rd.
Ascot Vale (Melbourne)
VIC 3032

# Contents

# What is a habitat?

A **habitat** is a place in nature.
Plants live in habitats.
Animals live in habitats.
Some animals make
homes in their habitats.

## Living and non-living things

There are **living things** in habitats.
Plants and animals are living things.
There are also **non-living things**
in habitats. Rocks, water, and
dirt are non-living things.

*living thing*          *non-living thing*

# Everything they need

Plants and animals need air, water, and food to stay alive. Everything they need is in their habitats. This bird has found food in its habitat.

## Habitat homes

Some animals have homes.
This baby fox has a home.
The log is its home. The
baby fox lives in the log.

# Backyard habitats

Back yards are habitats. Back yards
are places behind people's homes.
Back yards in the country may be
big. City back yards may be small.

## Look around

It is fun to spend time
in your back yard.
What living things do
you see in your yard?
What non-living things
do you see in your yard?

# Changing weather

Many places have four **seasons**. The seasons are spring, summer, autumn, and winter. As the seasons change, the weather also changes in backyard habitats.

*The weather is warm in spring. Many plants grow.*

*The weather is hot in summer. Flowers bloom on plants.*

The weather is cool in autumn.
Leaves fall from the trees.

The weather is cold in winter.
Snow covers the ground.

# Backyard plants

There are many plants in back yards. Trees are big plants. Apples grows on some trees. Bushes are smaller plants. Berries grow on some bushes. The ground in many back yards is covered with grass.

*trees*

*grass*

*bushes*

## Growing plants

Some people have flower gardens in their back yards. Bees and butterflies visit the flowers. Some people also have vegetable gardens in their back yards. They eat the vegetables they grow.

*flowers*

*vegetables*

# Plants make food

Living things need food. Plants make their own food. Plants use sunlight, air, and water to make food. Making food from sunlight, air, and water is called **photosynthesis**.

## Parts for making food

A plant gets sunlight through its leaves. It also gets air through its leaves. The plant gets water through its roots. The plant uses sunlight, air, and water to make food.

*Leaves take in sunlight.*

*Leaves take in air.*

*Roots take in water from soil.*

15

# Backyard animals

These animals live in back yards.
They can find food in back yards.
They can also find places to live.
Other animals also live in back yards.
Which animals live in your yard?

*raccoon*

*bird*

*squirrel*

*rabbit*

*wasp*

*skunk*

*deer*

17

# In the water

There is water in some back yards. Some back yards have **streams**. Streams have moving water. Other back yards have **ponds**. Ponds have still water. These people are feeding geese in a pond.

## Living near water

Some animals live near water.
Frogs and turtles live near water.
Sometimes frogs and turtles
visit back yards that
are near water.

# Babies in spring

Baby animals are born in the spring.
Baby rabbits hop around on the grass.
Young raccoons play in the trees.
Baby deer follow their mothers.
This baby deer drinks its mother's milk.

# Birds in trees

Birds build homes called **nests**. Baby birds chirp in their nests. They chirp to tell their mothers that they are hungry. Mother birds find them food. They put the food into the mouths of their babies.

# Plenty of food

Animals find food in their habitats.
Many backyard animals eat plants.
Animals that eat plants are called
**herbivores**. Squirrels are herbivores.
They eat seeds, flowers, and nuts.

## Eating animals

Some animals eat other animals. These animals are called **carnivores**. Pygmy owls are carnivores. They eat chipmunks and blue jays.

## Eating many foods

Some animals are **omnivores**. They eat both plants and other animals. Opossums are omnivores. They eat berries and grass. They also eat mice.

# Getting energy

*sun*

All living things need **energy**. Energy helps living things grow and move. Energy comes from the sun. Plants use the sun's energy to make food. Animals get energy by eating. A woodchuck is a herbivore. It gets energy by eating clover.

*clover*

*woodchuck*

## Energy for carnivores

A carnivore gets energy by eating other animals. A hawk is a carnivore. It gets energy by eating a woodchuck.

*hawk*

# Backyard homes

Some animals make homes in back yards. They sleep in their homes. Skunks dig homes under the ground. Rabbits make homes in bushes. Raccoons make homes in trees. A raccoon's home is called a **den**.

## Up and down

Some porcupines make homes on the ground. Other porcupines make homes in trees. Porcupines eat parts of trees. They eat bark, twigs, and leaves. Porcupines never eat the trees that are their homes!

# Sleepy days

There are some backyard animals you may not see in the daytime. These animals sleep during the day. They wake up at night to look for food. These baby foxes are sleeping in soft grass during the day.

## Sound asleep

These bats are sleeping in the daytime.
They are hanging from a tree branch.
They hold on tightly with their feet.
Most bats sleep in groups. How
many bats are in this group?

# Warm sleeps

In summer, you may see many animals in your back yard. In winter, you may see very few animals. Many animals sleep through the cold winter weather. They sleep in warm homes. This mouse has found a warm home.

## Waking up to eat

Chipmunks hide seeds and nuts for
the winter. They sleep through most
of winter. Sometimes they wake up
because they are hungry. They eat
the hidden food when they wake up.

# Words to know and Index

**animals**
pages 4, 5, 6, 7, 16-17, 19, 20, 22, 23, 24, 25, 26, 28, 30

**babies**
pages 20-21, 28

**energy**
pages 24-25

**food**
pages 6, 14, 15, 16, 21, 22-23, 24, 28, 31

**habitats**
pages 4, 5, 6, 7, 8, 10, 22

**homes**
pages 4, 7, 8, 21, 26-27, 30

**plants**
pages 4, 5, 6, 10, 12-13, 14, 15, 22, 23, 24

**sleep**
pages 26, 28-31

## Other index words

carnivores 23, 25
herbivores 22, 24
living things 5, 9, 14, 24
non-living things 5, 9
omnivores 23
photosynthesis 14
water 5, 6, 14, 15, 18-19

1 2 3 4 5 6 7 8 9 0   Printed in the U.S.A.   5 4 3 2 1 0 9 8 7 6